Stock Market 2021

A Beginners Guide To Invest In Stocks And Build Passive Income. Step- By-Step Strategies And Risk Management To Maximize Profit

[NOME DELLA SOCIETÀ]

Copyright 2021 - All rights reserved.

Table of Contents

Introduction

A swing trader doesn't need to sit at his computer watching the stock markets all day long, although you certainly can if that's an option for you and you like doing it. Swing traders can also start small and grow their business over time.

While substantial profits are attainable, it's not a get-rich-quick scheme and although it can be done on a part-time basis, we want you to start thinking of swing trading as a business from this point forward. The goal is to earn profits, and you can use those profits as ordinary income if you like or reinvest them to build your retirement account or some combination of the two. That is entirely up to you. But keep in mind one thing: very few people are going to make a millions in their first year and slide into retirement.

Swing trading can be a great way to earn a big profit in a short amount of time to the stock market. Start learning more about swing trading with this guidebook that's designed to provide you with concise information.

Chapter 1: Understanding the Stock market

The Origin and History of the Stock Market

Stock markets root its origin back to the period when the countries in the New World started to trade with each other. At this time, most of the pioneer merchants had the interest of starting a huge business but this was impossible because such businesses required huge amounts of capital that could not be raised by a single individual. This resulted in groups of different investors pooling their finances together to become business partners or co-owners. Using the shares contributed by every investor, joint-stock companies would be created. These companies were first used by the Dutch. The tremendous success of joint-stock companies proved to be a valuable business module. Particularly, many businesses that were either new or that was struggling with raising finances found this model to be very effective for promoting their growth. The first paper share to be issued was issued by the Dutch East India Company in 1602. With this exchangeable medium, investors and shareholders were able to conveniently trade (buy and sell) their stock with any other investors and shareholders.

This business model became very successful and this made the selling of stock shares to spread to outside Dutch to their neighboring countries like France, Spain, and Portugal. As time went by and nations accumulated wealth, this idea continued to spread until it reached England. This trade model became a big deal in the New World and saw the initiation of trading ventures. The Industrial Revolution further promoted its spread because it was almost impossible to begin private industry on your own. This business model was just perfect for industries and companies enabling them to acquire startup capital for their growth and expansion.

There was an influx of capital and the volume of shares in the market increased. This called for the need to have an organized marketplace where these shares could be bought and sold in an orderly manner. Stock traders, consequently, decided to hold a meeting in a London coffeehouse. The stock traders used this coffeehouse as their

11

marketplace. After conducting successful trades for a few years, it was time to have their own place with their identity. Therefore, in 1773, these traders buy the coffeehouse which they changed its name to "Stock exchange". This is how the first stock exchange was founded. They then named the building as the London Stock Exchange. The idea then made its way to America and in 1790 in Philadelphia, the first stock exchange was started.

More often, the term Wall Street is also used to refer to the Stock exchange. On May 17, 1792, the stock market on Wall Street was opened. It was located on the corner between Wall Street and Broadway. It involved 24 supply brokers who signed the Buttonwood Agreement. Later, on 8 March 1817, the name of the group was changed to the New York Stock and Exchange Board. They moved from their initial marketplace located in the 68 Wall Street to 40 Wall Street, New York. This was the birth of the organization would define the word's economic future.

Today we have many stock exchanges worldwide with each of them supplying different industries with the support necessary for their growth and expansion. Without the funds from the stock market, many of the revolutionary ideas we are seeing today would have never been a reality. Furthermore, the fundamental improvements we see being made to the existing products could have not been achieved. The stock market continues to create financial stability as well as personal wealth through private investment which allows companies to expand and individuals to raise their retirement funds/ other ventures.

What Is Stock?

A stock is a kind of securities. The stock we usually refer to refers to common stock, which is a share of ordinary rights in the company's management and that closely deals with the profit and distribution of property. Conceptually, stocks are stock certificates issued by a company limited by shares to investors when raising capital, representing the ownership of the company by its holders (i.e. shareholders).

For example, suppose a joint stock company has 100 shareholders, each of whom contributes 100,000 dollars, each of whom owns 1% of the company's ownership (equity). After the company has been approved by the competent authority, the stock is printed and handed over to the investor as a certificate of ownership. This is the original meaning of the stock.

Stocks can generally be transferred by way of sale and purchase. Shareholders can recover their investment through stock transfer, but they cannot ask the company to return their capital. Shareholders can buy and sell these stocks in the stock market, which constitutes the circulation of stocks in the hands of different investors and changes in ownership and holdings.

Stocks, like ordinary goods, have prices, can be bought and sold, and can be used as collateral. Anyone who owns these stocks can become a shareholder of the company. The relationship between shareholders and the company is not a creditor-debtor relationship. The shareholder is the owner of the company where the company has limited liability, risk-taking and sharing of income to the extent of its capital contribution.

Hence, stocks are securities issued by the stock company to investors to prove their shareholder rights and investment shares in the company and to obtain dividend income.

Types of Stock

The stock is issued by the joint stock company to the shareholders and is the shareholder certificate of the shareholder investment. The stocks are classified according to a variety of methods. According to the classification of dividends, it can be divided into several types. According to the enjoyment of voting rights, it can be divided into three types: single right, multiple powers, and no power.

Single-weight stocks

A single-weight stock means the shareholder has only one voting right.

13

Multi-right stocks

Multi-equity stocks are stocks that give the shareholder multiple voting rights per stock.

Unauthorized stocks

Unauthorized stocks are stocks that do not have voting rights.

In addition to classifying stocks according to the principle of classification, we often hear words such as "A shares" and "B shares" in daily life, which is based on how the stocks are issued.

Stock Listing Conditions

Stock listing refers to the legal act of publicly listing trading on the exchange after the stocks that have been issued have been approved by the stock exchange. The stock is listed as a "bridge" connecting stock issuance and stock trading.

The conditions for the termination of listing shares are as follows.

1) The listed company's total share capital and shareholding distribution have changed, and no longer have listing conditions. The listing conditions cannot be met within the time limit set by the stock exchange.

2) The listed company does not disclose its financial accounting report in accordance with the regulations or has False records of financial accounting reports and has refused to correct them.

3) The listed company has suffered consecutive losses for three years and failed to resume profitability in the following year.

4) The listed company is dissolved or declared bankrupt.

How the Stock Market Works

Most stocks are traded in the various stock exchanges in the world. These exchanges are regulated by the government agencies responsible for securities and exchange in

14

the countries hosting these exchanges. The government agencies protect those investing in the publicly listed companies from financial fraud and help maintain the operation of the stock exchanges.

There are three major players in the stock market – the investment banks, stockbrokers, and investors. The investment banks are responsible for handling the initial public offering of companies when they decide to offer their shares for public investment. These banks are approached by these companies and become their underwriters. As an underwriter, the investment bank will use its research on the company to determine the guaranteed minimum price per share and how much of the ownership the company is willing to relinquish to the public as shares. In return, the investment bank handles the initial issue of shares to the public for a fee. Usually, large institutional investors, like mutual fund companies, purchase shares sold during an IPO. After that, all trading of the shares occurs in the stock exchange – the secondary market.

In the exchange, stockbrokers buy and sell the stocks according to the order of their clients – the investors. Stockbrokers may also act as financial advisors, so their clients make the best decisions according to their goals. They often offer research on publicly traded companies and provide a forecast on overall market index or stock price performance. This service is offered since stockbrokers want their clients to succeed in their investments and trades. If they experience success in their stock trades, they will likely transact more trades and remain as their customer.

Different Types of Stock Trading

Once, you have decided to invest in the stock market; you should set your pre-determined trading objectives. According to how your objectives are to be met, the type of trading can be chosen. You should start zeroing down all the types of stock trading, and notice, that all these types have their unique abilities. Different types of stock trading are used for different types of stock. You should be able to do conduct proper market research, to understand the stock market psychology. This would help you pick out the best option.

Short term trading

This kind of trading means the period ranges from a day to a few days, to a week or a few weeks, which means, best for veteran traders, as they would have excessive knowledge on how to deal with the trade-in such a crucial period. Hence, it isn't appropriate for beginners, as you may have to deal with uncertainty and deep losses.

Market Order

This is one of the simplest types of stock trading. You're supposed to ask your broker to select the stock, and then buy at the current rate. No analysis or research work is required for this trading. It has a flexible time duration, as the stock might be bought for a few days or extended for months.

Though, it has the lowest commission amount. The overall idea is to gain enough profit to cover the commission cost and the stock holding cost. So, there is less risk. Considering this type of trading would be quite useful, but it doesn't have the highest profit gains and would require a broker. Lack of research and analysis would mean a lack of knowledge of the stock market, which is more of a disadvantage for you.

Intra-day trading

This trading is initiated in a span of a single trading day. All existing market positions are squared off within the trading hours. Higher returns are guaranteed, and the overall amount of return is linked to the additional minute, which increases the additional profit. But since it requires technical analysis, it is more suitable to such analysts and experts, who would know how the complexity works.

High-frequency trading

In this, the bid is to be manipulated, and price asked at a great speed. A small profit is earned as trades occur every day. Another complexity which can't be handled by beginners, due to lack of research work and analysis.

Swing Trading

As you get familiar with this type of stock trading, you'll see the rapid price fluctuations in the market. This swing trade takes advantage of overnight price swings of stocks. You need to predict the accurate extent of price fluctuation, which would determine the profit margin. There is no high leverage and there is a higher degree of return potential, but the risk is high due to the additional margins. The fluctuations and movements of the price should be analyzed carefully.

If you chose this trading type, you would have to invest a lot of capital, which would mean margin risk and higher liabilities.

Chapter 2: How to Get Started with the Stock

Deciding on how to invest in stocks

There are numerous ways on how to invest in stocks. All of these methods have advantages and disadvantages, but every your situation is different. What's good for you may lead to a problematic situation for another. Considering the period and market value, while looking for stocks to invest in, is highly recommended.

Sometimes, the market may be going through a smooth and steady path that your emotional aspects may get in the way. You may invest in expensive stocks due to the success of the market. On the other hand, in a poorly performing market during situations like inflation, you may start to sell off your stocks.

So how can you decide where to invest? First off, you need to analyze how much a certain method of investment would be affected by the level of risk and potential losses. If the risk is too high, but the gains from it would be more fruitful, you would know what step to take. Such decision making requires proper research of all the methods, and a proper understanding of how much would be at stake, in different situations.

Know what you want to achieve

What you can do with the stock market depends on what you want to achieve out of it. Are you aiming to use it to replace your income and quit your job? Are you going to use it to build wealth alongside your job? Are you going to use it to build-up funds for retirement?

Each of these goals would require a different approach to the stock market compared to the other two. For example, replacing the income from your work would require a more aggressive strategy than a strategy for building up your wealth or retirement fund. This also applies to the frequency of trades that you do within the week.

Straighten out your finances

You must consider your job security, your income, any outstanding debt, and other financial obligations you have, your current and future expenses, your cash savings, and your household budget. This will provide you with a clear picture of your finances and help you make a more informed decision if you have the budget to get started now. If not, you can build up capital for the stock market with your job. Either way, you'll have a better starting point and will not put in money that you cannot afford.

Knowing your financial situation will also help you keep track of your expenses moving forward. It can help prevent unnecessary expenses that negatively affect your funds for trading or, worse, cause you to take on debt.

Save up for emergencies

Before you even get started, you need to save money for emergencies. You will not put this into investments that have the risk of loss in value or capital. The most that you can do with this money is to put it in a money market fund or certificates of deposits.

Do not quit your job

The worst mistake that you can do when starting out in the stock market is quitting your job. It's easy to get carried with how much earning potential the stock market has in store for anyone. But, before you even get to that point, you'll have to learn the ropes first and gain enough experience to create good results. And, as they say, the only way to get that experience is by doing, which comes with making mistakes. This could mean losing money depending on your strategy and falling short in terms of achieving goals in time or on target.

Familiarize yourself with the stock market

You are already doing this by reading this book. This book presents you with the basics that you need to know to get started and answers the frequently asked question about it. But there is a lot more than you can do.

You can get a better start in the stock market by learning from successful stock investors and traders. You can find books by authors who already went through what you'll be going through. You will essentially learn from their experiences, successes, and failures, which will help you achieve your goals faster. Some of the best books go beyond how to do research, create strategies, or make a trade, and include the psychological aspects of trading in the stock market.

Choosing a Stockbroker

You cannot trade or invest in the stock market if you can't buy or sell shares in the stock market. To do so, you would have to set-up an account with a stockbroker that will facilitate these transactions for you. Like any service provider, not all stockbrokers are equal. You would want a broker that can provide you the best service without charging you over-the-top fees. Here are the considerations you must take when choosing your broker:

Suitability to your needs

You know your objectives about buying and selling shares in the stock market. Consequently, you have an idea of how you would be doing your transactions while trying to achieve these objectives. Brokers would have different features, and it's vital that your choice can provide what you require. Salient features to consider include charts, financial data, analyst support, educational resources, broker assistance, and customer service channels.

Client protection and insurance

You must make sure that the broker you choose follows the law and provides protection for its clients. It should have a relevant regulatory body (such as FINRA in the United States) to authorize its operations to ensure that it provides a fair and honest service to investors. The broker should also provide investor protection insurance for customer cash claims, and deposit insurance for deposit products if the company fails. They should also protect your personal information in their systems and offer two-factor login authentication. Lastly, the broker should have a form of guarantee protection that will reimburse losses caused by fraudulent activities.

Consider Minimum deposit amounts and fees

Most stockbrokers require a minimum deposit to open an account. A basic stock trading account will typically require a minimum balance of $500 to $1,000. But if you want to open a margin account, you will have to prepare a relatively higher amount and must consider their interest rate for making a trade on margin.

Trading platform

If you can, test the platform before you start using the broker to buy and sell shares. It does not matter if it's a web-based or app-based. What you're looking for is a platform that lets you place an order smoothly. It should let you trade the securities that you need to trade and create orders that you require for your goals and schedule.

The trading platform should also provide real-time data. You should be able to set-up watchlists and alerts so you can get notifications, preferably via text. You should also consider if you would require trading in extended hours and if the broker would charge extra for it.

Look at the charting features available on the platform. See if it plots the data that you want to see and if you find it easy to do so. Do not settle for a broker that lack any of the basic indicators - volume, simple moving averages, RSI, Bollinger bands, stochastics, and MACD.

Lastly, you should find it easy to use the brokerage's platform. It should only take you more than 30 minutes to get used to browsing the different menus and pages and grasp how to create and execute trade orders. At the very least, the broker should provide a short video tutorial on how to use the platform.

Client education

Even if you can find the generic information in this book and other sources online, brokers are a valuable source of information for stock trading. Market updates and fundamental data can provide great insight from experts that will equip you to create better decisions. Of course, this depends on the quality and capability of their sources and staff.

Ease of transaction with the broker

Make sure that you can easily add or withdraw money from your brokerage account. Long turnaround times can make you miss sudden opportunities even if you schedule your deposits regularly. Moreover, you should choose a broker that will let you add or withdraw funds with the methods available to you – bank or wire transfer, debit or ATM card, or linked bank accounts.

Customer service

Choose a broker that provides access to customer service quickly and easily. This is even more significant when you are just starting out and require additional assistance in the beginning. Check if they provide the customer service channel that you prefer.

Buying and selling shares of stock

Once you have an account with a broker, you can start buying stocks in an exchange. There is no minimum to how much you must buy to invest in a stock. But it is best to buy in lots since there are charges added on top of the investment you're making. This is why it's advised to purchase at least a single lot size for a given stock.

A lot is a fixed increment that stocks are traded in the market. These increments often come in 100s while higher-priced stocks come in 10s. You can still set orders with an increment below the number of lots for the stock since companies can split shares or issue stock dividends.

Trades are created through the orders entered in the order entry interface of your broker's platform. These orders indicate the stock and number of shares that you want to buy, and the ask or bid price for each one. Once you submit your order in your broker's order entry interface, the broker will facilitate this for you electronically. Orders will push through when there are matching sell and bid orders in the market.

When the orders push through, buyers receive their new shares and have the cost of the shares and the associated fees deducted from their accounts. For sellers, the broker deducts the relevant fees from the proceeds before crediting what remains to the seller's account.

What you earn from stocks sold, that increased in price, is subject to tax. The rate would depend on how long you held the stock. If you held the stock for more than a year, the proceeds would be subject to long-term capital gains rates depending on your taxable income. But, if you held it for less than a year, the proceeds would be subjected to ordinary income tax rates depending on your taxable income.

Methods of investment

As talked about in the previous passage, we know that all methods would have certain effects, but at the end, the success relies on how much risk you're ready to take, as well as how much knowledge you have in stock marketing. If you're into a more modern and technological way of business, then you should know, online buying of stocks is a thing.

Although, it is only recommended if you're well aware of how the stock market operates, and can give useful advice to yourself, as this one doesn't involve any advices to be given, so you're on your own. Also, it's far riskier, as you are charged only a flat fee for each transaction. Also, to mention, it's time-consuming, as you would have to train yourself until you're confident enough to take the next step.

Investment Club

The next method which you can consider is through the investment clubs. You meet a lot of people who may be going through the same situation you are, and people who can give professional and financial advices. Other people's experiences can make you learn a lot too. It's affordable and can help you to understand and differentiate between different market situations. Increased involvement and investing in stocks through this can help you gain a new perspective and a sense of direction.

Full-Service Broker

Then we have a full-service broker. Know that this is an expensive method, as the fees paid to your broker are quite high, but the excess information makes up for it.

The broker will help you with the recommendation and advice on how to take the next step, and the precaution measure to be taken while looking for a good financial advisor. This leads to increased business know-how, more knowledge about the stock market, and increased confidence in your decisions.

The trends in the market should be considered at all points

Consumer taste and changes in choices should be properly analyzed, and the reasons behind them should be known. If the owners of the business have enough knowledge about this, and the managers are efficient enough to make this happen, it means your potential risk may be lower.

As a beginner, it is essential to consider how the country's economy is doing. Inflation would mean that there can be a sudden downfall in the trends and greater risk of bankruptcy. The time of investing should be carefully chosen. That being said, it is proven that there never is the perfect time to invest in the market. Comparison of different timings is significant. This also depends on the type of goods or services being offered. The price elasticity of demand and supply would help you find out how the market will do during inflation.

Moreover, for long term success, the growth of the company needs to be taken into consideration. Over time, how much the company has grown, and what is the difference between its earnings when it started fresh, and what is it now? This determines the stability of the company you plan to invest in. Many businesses go through ups and downs, but the major ones are what you should avoid at all cost. The strength of the industry and how well it does in the market will show how much potential the company has for long-term success.

Coming on to the other fundamental aspects, the debt and the equity ratio needs to be measured beforehand. If the company is in too much debt and isn't making enough profit to pay it off, it would call for liquidation, which means selling off the assets of the company. You won't be left with anything in this case.

Chapter 3: Picking Winning Stocks

Sit down to ponder on your plan and take a look at the mix of stock types you've decided will make up your portfolio. Now we'll begin to look for stocks to fill them. Here are the things you should look for in every company you're considering investing in.

What to Look For

These factors work together to determine the overall value and promise of a company. All or most of these need to be strong to make buying a share of ownership in the company a good idea. These factors together will give you an overall picture of the health of the company now and a clear window into its future.

Revenue

This is the first line on an income statement. Revenue is how much money a company is bringing in the door, not accounting for expenses or any other adjustment. When looking at revenue, what you're hoping to see is a steady increase over a decent period. Within the same year, quarterly reports may fluctuate wildly depending on the type of company, but you want to see a year-to-year incline in revenue overall.

P/E

This abbreviation stands for Price-Earnings Ratio. A lot of experts consider this the principal number to look at when considering purchasing a stock. While that is debatable, it is certainly very significant. The P/E is a single number representing the result of some simple math. First, the company's overall earnings are divided by the number of shares outstanding, giving the Share Earnings. Then, the price of the stock on the market is divided by that number. Here's an example:

Company X earned $500,000 last year and has 10,000 shares outstanding. This means its share earnings are $50. If the stock is selling for $200 per share, the P/E of this stock is 4.

Whether you're looking for a low or higher P/E is based on the amount of risk vs reward you're looking to assume with the purchase. If a stock is a good value, its P/E should be low compared to other companies in the same industry.

Net Earnings

This is the revenue minus all the expenses the company incurs. It's easy to think that a higher net earnings line always means the company is in a better position than one with a lower net earnings, but this isn't necessarily true.

Some reasons a company might show a low net earnings but still be strong are restructuring, major innovation or product development, and changes in management. These could improve the earnings for the upcoming years greatly. Net earnings are a key factor, but it's just as important to look at it in the context of the other facts about the company, and the industry at large.

ROE

Return on Equity is the measure of how well the company is using the money that it makes to improve share value. It is calculated by dividing the net income for the full year by the shareholder's equity (the total of all assets minus the total of all liabilities.) Note that preferred stock should also be subtracted as a liability. It is not part of common equity. This number should again be low relative to other companies in the same industry.

Debt Ratios

This is the ratio of all debt to all assets. You'll usually see it notated as a percentage or decimal. A high percentage doesn't always mean the company isn't being managed well. As with ROE, look at several years averaged together and at other companies within the same industry.

Future Earnings

Obviously, we don't have a crystal ball, but we can get an idea of how a company will probably do soon. Companies publish "forecast future earnings." Be aware, though: these are the opinions from within the company and tend to be overly optimistic. In order to glean a picture closer to reality, look at forecasts from the past and compare them to the actual performance, and that will give you an idea of how far from the mark the reports tend to be.

Competition

In all these measures, you've been comparing each value to the same value of other companies in the industry. While you have that in front of you, take a closer look at the competition. If they have new products that look promising and innovative, that could make the stock you're looking at less attractive. Most importantly, looking thoroughly at the competition will give you a clear picture of the landscape in which you are looking to invest.

How to Properly Research A Company's Stock Prior to Investing

It's essential to do a proper research first regarding the company stock that you would like to purchase. It's foolish to simply dive in and purchase some stocks without doing proper investigation prior to investing. For all you know, you may never have a chance to recover everything that you have lost.

Here are some of the places where you can get reliable information regarding your target company:

1. Investor Relations section of the Company's Website

2. Morning Star's website

3. Yahoo Finance

4. Google Finance

5. SEDAR (System for Electronic Document Analysis and Retrieval)

6. Securities Exchange Commission website

Where to Find Information

When a company goes public, allowing its shares to be traded on stock exchanges, it has to file reports on its earnings and the state of its financial health in order to stay in good standing with the Security Exchange Commission. This is great news for us because a lot of the information we need to buy with confidence is contained in those forms. There are three commonly published forms, the 10-K, the 10-Q and the 8K. These all contain different information for different periods of time but looking at all or some of them will give you an insight into the following aspects of the company.

The 10-K is released once a year and contains the fiscal information for that year. It is audited by an outside accounting firm.

A 10-Q contains some of the same information, but covers only a 90-day time-period and isn't usually independently audited

An 8-K is not released on a set schedule, but whenever major changes are going on within the company. Good things like acquisitions or deals the company has made are included, as well as bad news like SEC investigations. Any material event that could affect the shareholders is an inducement for the release of an 8-K, and it isn't unusual for several to be filed throughout the year.

Honestly, these forms do not make for the most exciting reading. They contain a lot of dry facts with no pitch or polish. That's what makes them so valuable for investors, though! The facts are exactly what you need to decide.

Stock Screeners

This is a ton of information to look at for each stock you want to buy, but there's really no way to be a smart investor without doing it. Luckily, software specifically made to filter through the mountain of data available can help. Stock Screeners allow you to set the parameters of stocks you're looking for, such as relative risk, debt ratios, stock type, and a lot of the other determining factors we've discussed. Then, it only shows you the relevant information for stocks that fit those parameters. This can be an invaluable time saver, especially when building your portfolio.

Analysts

Television and the internet are full of opinions on investing. While some of these sources are invaluable, a lot of them are better at getting attention than providing useful advice. Finding analysts whose opinions you respect and whose values align with your own may not be easy, but it will be worth it because you'll have something to check your gut instincts against.

Chapter 4: How Is Stock Price Determined?

Now that we have covered the basics about the stock market, it's time we analyze some of the finer details like how the stock prices are determined. Stock prices go up and down all the time, but do you know why? If you want to pinpoint the exact reason behind the price of a stock, then I am telling you this right now – it's impossible. There are not one but plenty of factors acting behind the price of a single stock, and it isn't influenced singularly by any of them. But yes, with a little effort, you can easily understand the basics behind the price determination of stocks.

Before that, let me give you a brief intro into the capital markets –

Primary markets are set up by the capital markets so that a company can raise money through an IPO. An initial price is set up after consulting the investment bankers, and then investors start lining up for the stocks of that company.

Now that the IPO is done, the stocks have been bought by the common investors who can then, in turn, buy or sell them in the *secondary market*. This happens in different stock exchanges. Now, here the price is influenced by demand and supply. The ultimate price of the shares will be decided by the bid and ask price. The ask price is referred to as the minimum price that the seller will accept to get the concerned security. The bid price is the highest price that the buyers are ready to pay for purchasing the concerned shares.

Some other factors that should be factored in when you're discussing the price or when the price is determined are as follows –

The first factor is the earnings of the company in question. I will agree that the stock price is not influenced by this factor every day, but before any investment decisions are finalized, the earnings of the company are something that will be looked into by analysts.

Institutional investors and the trades they perform is the second factor that you should have a look at. Hedge funds, mutual funds, or even pension plans might be included in this.

Thirdly, the market conditions certainly influence the price of stocks. Let us say; there is some bad or good market event, then it can directly influence the price of the stocks as well. For example, in 2008, when there was a financial crisis, there was a drop of 37% in the S&P 500.

How to Read Stock Quotes?

Stock quotes can seem hard to read, not only to a beginner but even for a seasoned trader. There is a combination of numbers that you need to figure out. The different elements that are present in a stock quote have been explained below and once you know them, reading a stock quote should become easier –

Company Name

If you see a stock table, you'll notice that there are so many shares, and all of them are to be fitted in that space, so no company uses its full name. To get over this space crunch, companies have specific symbols, and you must know them. You can search them on the internet or the trading platform of your broker.

Stock Price

This is quite obvious that your stock quote will include the stock price. The price basically keeps fluctuating not only by the day but also every minute. They remain constant only when the markets have been closed.

High/Low

With time, as more and more trades are conducted, the live share prices keep fluctuating. The valuation of a stock decreases when it is sold, and it increases when it is bought. Thus, the price of a share is affected accordingly. So, the stock quote makes it easier for an investor to compare, and because of that, both the lowest and highest price hit by the stock on that particular day is mentioned in the stock quote.

Close

When the market closes, the stock prices also stop changing. So, the close here refers to the closing price, and so it will tell you about the last price at which the stock was traded on that day. If you look at this specific value when the market is open, you'll be looking at the closing price for the previous day.

Net Change

Since the stock quote mentions the closing price, you can imagine how easy it becomes to automatically calculate the change in price that took place. Both an absolute value and a change of percentage is mentioned when this change is stated. If there has been an increase in the price of a stock from what it was the previous day, then it's a positive change and vice-versa. Green is used to mark a positive change, whereas a negative change is indicated by red.

52-Week High/Low

Here, the number 52 refers to the 52 weeks in a year or simply one year, and this will represent the lowest and highest prices of that stock in one year. The investor will then be able to find out how the stock has performed over a broader time-period.

Dividend Details

As you already know, for the investors, dividends serve as the primary income source, and for anyone who is in the market for the long-term, this information is valuable. That is why the dividend yield is something that you'll find mentioned in certain stock quotes.

PE Ratio

When the price of the stock of the company is divided by the earnings per share, you get the PE ratio and the market sentiment is what dictates this ratio. You will often get it in the stock quotes.

Volume

Lastly, the demand for the stocks dictates the volume of trade of the stocks of a company. This section will show you exactly how many stocks of the company have changed hands.

Chapter 5: Buying and Selling Stocks

There are several factors to consider when picking winning stocks. Realizing that you aren't always going to get it 100% right is important. Even the best investors make mistakes. The key to success is picking yourself up and moving on when mistakes happen and focusing on your overall portfolio rather than on individual wins and losses. Thinking long-term always helps as well.

Let's go over some of the key points when picking winning stocks.

Understanding Company Value

New investors may have a gut-level understanding that Apple and Google are valuable stocks. But it's essential to really understand what makes a stock valuable. Investing in hunches can produce profits sometimes, but in most cases, it will lead investors sideways or even toward losses. It's important to combine your gut-level feelings about different investments with the cold, hard facts that we can derive from doing an analysis.

Aside: Penny Stocks

Some penny stocks trade on the major exchanges, others trade "over the counter" and are called pink sheets. The bottom line is that you should stay away from penny stocks. It's certainly within reach for a company with stock prices this low to turn things around and experience tremendous growth, but it is a rare event.

Company Fundamentals

The next factor to consider when picking a winning stock is to look at company fundamentals. This will include having a look at the financial statements of the company, which they are required to make available if they are a publicly traded company on a major stock exchange. These reports will help you analyze the cash flow, assets, liabilities, and revenue of the company. You'll want to use them to determine the company's profitability and outlook going forward.

Price-to-Earnings Ratio

Price-to-earnings ratio compares the price of a share to the earnings per share. If a company has solid fundamentals and a high level of earnings per share, a low price-to-earnings ratio is a signal that the stock is available at a discount. Sometimes investors are behind the times in finding good value, and so the stock will be low priced because of lack of demand. That situation won't last forever, so if you find a stock that fits this description, it can be a good addition to your portfolio. A stock with a low ratio is probably well-placed to appreciate in value over time.

Aligning Stock Picks with Your Investment Goals

As we'll see, it's valued to develop an investment strategy that helps you realize your financial goals. You might be late getting in on investing, and so aggressive growth through strong stock appreciation will be more significant. Alternatively, you might be looking to build a safe investment income portfolio, preserving wealth and earning an income from it rather than seeking out rapid growth. No matter what your investment goals are, picking stocks that align with your goals is as significant as looking at fundamentals and other characteristics like market capitalization.

Do Your Research

Doing your research is important. It will help you pick good companies that are going to help you build wealth. Doing research will also help you determine the best time to enter or exit a position and meet your goals. A winning investor studies the companies they invest in as well as the markets.

Market order

This is an order that you place if you wish to buy a share immediately and at the best price. Here, you will be guaranteed of the order's immediate execution.

With a market order, you'll buy shares at the price closest to the posted ask price. The same is true if you wish to sell shares. Your shares will sell at the market at a price closest to the nearest posted bid. This is a great way, as an individual trader to get your orders executed immediately. You may not know the exact price, but you can expect to pay or receive a price as close to the bid or ask price as possible.

Limit order

This is an order that sets both the maximum and minimum prices that you're willing to pay for or sell your shares. But there are always commissions involved and they are usually higher for limit orders but lower for market orders.

Broker

A broker is an individual or firm with direct access to the stock markets. Brokers enable members of the public to trade at the stock market via their platforms. So, if you wish to trade and invest at the stock market, you will most likely need to contact a broker. Fortunately, you do not need to visit their offices because all this is possible online.

Simply identify a suitable broker, open an account, provide basic information, answer a couple of questions, and then begin trading as soon as possible. You will need to fund your account prior to buying stocks. Thus, find out the different funding options available and determine the amount you wish to deposit. Brokers often have certain requirements such as a minimum deposit amount and so on. Make sure you are aware of this in order to remain compliant.

Diversification

As an investor, you should not invest all your money in a single stock. This is very similar to putting all your eggs in one basket. Accordingly, identify several stocks from different industries such as financial services sector, industrial, automotive, oil and gas, transport, and so on. If you can identify some good shares in some of these sectors, then you'll improve your chances for success at the stock markets. Statistics indicate that diversified portfolios are much more successful and earn more money that single stock portfolios.

Diversification also saves you from imminent loss should anything negative happen. People have been known to lose their investments for lack of diversification. For instance, let us assume you purchase Boeing stocks and shortly thereafter major incidents involving airplane crashes happen. The stock would plummet in value and you would lose most of your investments.

Stock Prices

When you invest in stocks, you need to be on the lookout for price changes regularly. Prices rise and fall based on a variety of factors. For instance, when interest rates fall, the economy will have a positive outlook and stock prices will very likely rise. On the other hand, when an industry specific incident happens or the economy falls into recession, the prices are bound to fall. In general, the stock market is a static entity and prices are always falling and rising. You should know when you want to benefit from this regular rise and all in price, also known as volatility. You can benefit greatly by buying stocks when the price is low then selling when prices go up.

Building an Investment Portfolio

As an investor, the best approach is diversification. Diversification means investing your funds in different securities. This is highly advisable because of the inherent and underlying risks posed by the markets. It's a fact that the price or value of stocks keeps changing almost all the time. Risking everything on a single venture is not a smart thing to do. Diversification means no matter what happens, you can still be profitable.

Therefore, to invest wisely, you will need to develop or come up with a suitable investment portfolio. It's easy to imagine an investment portfolio as where all your investments are held. A portfolio is in other ways similar to a safe that stores crucial personal or business documents. However, unlike a safe, it is more of a concept rather than a tangible product.

When you diversify your investments into a portfolio, it means that you will own a myriad of assets. These assets could be exchange traded funds or ETFs, mutual funds, bonds, stocks, and many others. So, it is best to approach diversification of a portfolio with a well-thought-out plan and not haphazardly.

Principles of Building a Portfolio

We can define portfolio management as an approach of balancing rewards and risks. In order to meet your investment goals, you'll need to invest in a wide variety of products including SMAs, REITs, close-end funds, ETFs and others. It's a very good idea and highly recommended to have an investment plan and determine what your end goal is especially when there are such numerous options available.

Portfolio management often means different things to different investors. Think about a young person fresh from college and on his first job. Such a person views portfolio management as a way of growing investments and providing a pretty decent amount over time for future use. On the other hand, a person not so young who has been working or running a business for a while will view things differently.

Such a person will view portfolio management as an excellent chance of holding on to their wealth possibly accumulated over the years. There are different ways of organizing and planning portfolio management. A portfolio manager should be able to handle the various needs that different investors have when coming up with a diversified portfolio. Hence, individualized approach is the highly advised option. Here are some basic principles of developing a portfolio.

First it is advisable to note the availability of numerous options. This means that there are plenty of investment vehicles to choose from. Thus, a client or investor needs to determine whether they wish to create wealth over time, put away funds for future use, generate a regular income, and so on. This way, a suitable investment plan will be attainable. Such a plan should incorporate appetite for risk, time period, and similar aspects.

Analysis

Investors need to learn a lot about analysis. We have fundamental analysis and technical analysis. Fundamental analysis is great for investors. This is the kind of analysis that reveals useful information about a company. It looks at the company's performance, finances, outlook, its management team, and much more. The kind of information revealed by fundamental analysis is crucial as it enables investors to decide on which companies to invest in and which stocks to buy.

On the other hand, technical analysis provides details about a stock. If you want to know how a stock will perform in the coming days, then you will use history and charts to determine its future movement. This is more popular with traders than it is with investors. Although, learning how to perform both fundamental analysis and technical analysis is advisable. It will give you an advantage so that you can become a better investor.

Stock Market Information

There is a lot of information that you'll need if you are to invest successfully. As an investor, you may have to spend a lot of time using some tools such as charts and technical analysis. These help in identifying trends and trading or investment opportunities. Fortunately, a lot of this information is made readily available by your stockbroker. So, check whatever tools and information they provide that will make your work as an investor easier.

Chapter 6: Key Stock Market Indexes

Index investing uses the approach of diversifying an investor's funds into a variety of stocks. The aim is to ensure that the portfolio's outcome or performance mirrors the performance of the entire stock exchange. The reason why investors love this approach and why experts recommend it is because studies have shown, that this performs much better than most strategies, especially in the long-term.

The index investing strategy is usually succeeded by mutual funds' investments and sometimes ETFs or exchange traded funds which are specifically designed to match popular stock indexes such as the FTSE 100 and the S&P 500.

Remember that growth typically wells up from a low interest rate atmosphere. Basically, when companies begin earning profits and interest rates are low, then the growth strategy will pick, and the investment strategy will be successful. Most stocks will continue to gain in price long after this bullish period comes to an end.

Although, these stocks are likely to take a beating should things go wrong or when the economy tanks. Therefore, keep this in mind when applying this strategy. Hopefully, it's becoming apparent why it is advisable to use a combination of strategies. Focus on at least two of the main strategies if not all three.

In short, you need to eventually be able to try out these different strategies, discover which ones suit your investment needs, and then finally choose the one you prefer the most. It is highly likely that any investment strategy you adopt will change in due course of time. You should not worry about this because it's completely normal and almost every investor does it.

However, you should focus on overseeing your investment approach so that you can determine exactly how your portfolio will be affected. This way, you will comfortably emerge the winner and your portfolio will enjoy excellent performance over the years. Sometimes traders even combine all the three distinct approaches in order to maximize on incomes and minimize losses.

Chapter 7: Essential Technical Indicators

Any trader looking to trade or invest at the securities markets and be profitable needs to learn about technical indicators. These guide traders, so they know the best points to enter, exit, and take profit points. Using indicators, a trader will benefit from accurate, reliable, and profitable trades. To understand more about technical indicators, we need to start from the beginning.

Technical indicators can be defined as mathematical computations worked out systematically using the volumes, price, and other factors that are essential to traders who rely on technical analysis.

Analysts often use historical data related to a security they are interested in. Historical data is believed to be a strong predictor or indicator of future events. Using this analysis, a trader can predict with high levels of accuracy the expected price movements of a stock. Some of the more popular technical indicators are Bollinger Bands, moving averages, RSI or relative strength index, Stochastic, and money flow index.

How Technical Indicators Function

Technical analysis is generally adapted by traders and investors in order to analyze and evaluate various investments then note any trading opportunities available. This is only possible where stocks have historical data available and easily accessible. The statistics collected over a few years, is analyzed and the information used for trading purposes.

Technical analysts focus on trading signals, price movements and related patters, as well as various charting tools. These are used to provide information about the strengths or weaknesses of a given stock.

Technical Indicators

Technical indicators are mostly used by traders and analysts because the outcomes they provide relate to short-term volume and price movements. They are very popular with short-term traders but are also used by long-term investors. There are generally two types of indicators. These two types are overlays and oscillators.

Oscillators:

These are technical indicators that move or oscillate between a maximum and minimum points. These points are found below or above a price chart. Examples of oscillators are moving averages, scholastic, and RSI.

Overlays:

Overlays are technical indicators that tend to operate on similar scales where analysts indicate prices onto prices found on a stock chart.

In general, traders tend to use numerous tools in order to check, confirm, and double confirm the accuracy of their analysis. While there are thousands of different tools out there to choose from, traders need to identify the ones that work well for them otherwise they will simply confuse themselves. Sometimes it is advisable to choose from among different tools so that only the most suitable ones are used. These can also be used on automated trading platforms to make the trading process easier and more accurate.

Summary – Technical Indicators

It is now clear that technical indicators are calculations that derive from the volume, price, and interest of a stock. Traders and analysts basically watch out for certain technical indicators using a security's price data if and where that is applicable. The technical indicators that result from a technical analysis process can be categorized.

Common Technical Indicators

Traders need to lookout for the most effective technical indicators out there. This is a key aspect because it will have a huge effect on how trends in the stock markets will be interpreted. Those who make wise choices will be happy and profitable traders and will smile all the way to the bank. Those that do not choose wisely will not fare well and probably lose their funds.

Most novice traders tend to go with the flow. They do not have much experience necessary to determine the most suitable indicators. As such, they stuff their trades with indicators, and this tends to cause confusion. It's much better to manually identify indicators and then choose a few that are most effective or most suitable.

Indicators work best when they are used to simplify the analytical process. As such, a trader or analyst needs to identify their own style and then find about two to five distinct tools that suit his style of trading and research. This way, the analysis process will become clear. In essence, there are about five different types of indicators. These are listed below.

- Trend indicators: These indicators are lagging indicators and basically analyze or assess a market's direction. The aim is to find or identify the direction of the trend. This can be upwards, downwards, and even sideways.

- Momentum indicators: We also have momentum indicators. These are leading indicators and they analyze the rate at which stock prices change over some time.

- Relative strength indicators: We have relative strength indicators which check oscillations where there is pressure to purchase or sell.

- Mean reversion indicator: This is a lagging indicator and is used by traders to confirm just how far the value swing of a share will travel or move before there emerges a counter impulse which then introduces a retracement.

- Volume indicators: These can be both leading and lagging indicators. Their main purpose is to add up individual trades and then determine which one between the bulls and bears is in control.

In conclusion, we can determine that leading indicators point to the direction of the price and lagging indicators inform about the various conditions once the price or value starts to move.

You can also use the RSI to identify oversold and overbought conditions. It is vital that you can identify these conditions as you trade because you will easily identify corrections and reversals. Sometimes securities are overbought at the markets, when this situation occurs, it means that there is a potential trend reversal and usually the emerging trend is bearish. This is often a market correction. Basically, when a security is oversold, it signals a correction or bullish trend reversal but when it's overbought, it introduces a bearish trend reversal.

Traders tend to use numerous tools in order to check, confirm, and double confirm the accuracy of their analysis. While there are thousands of different tools out there to choose from, traders need to identify the ones that work well for them otherwise they will simply confuse themselves.

Sometimes it's advisable to choose from among different tools so that only the most suitable ones are used. These can also be used on automated trading platforms to make the trading process easier and more accurate. Technical indicators need to be calibrated to the most suitable numerical inputs.

200 and 50-Day EMA

Some of the top technical indicators include the moving averages. We have the 50-day and the 200-day exponential moving averages. These are found embedded across the same panel together with price bars such as intraday, weekly, and daily. A moving average is an indicator that focuses on the price action of a stock over a given period.

The reason why the 200-day and the 50-day exponential moving averages or EMAs are chosen is because they happen to be a lot more sensitive and responsive compared to SMA or simple moving averages. In basic terms, the 50-day EMA investigates the average price of a stock. And the 200-day exponential moving average investigates the average price of a stock in the long-term.

Bollinger Bands

One of the most critical indicators that you'll need is the Bollinger band indicator. It's a technical indicator that performs two crucial purposes. The first is to identify sections of the market that are overbought and oversold. The other purpose is to check the market's volatility.

This indicator consists of 3 distinct moving averages. There is a central one which is an SMA or Simple Moving Average and then there two on each side of the SMA. These are also moving averages but are plotted on either side of the central SMA about 2 standard deviations away.

RSI – Relative Strength Index

Another crucial indicator that is commonly used by swing traders and other traders is the RSI or Relative Strength Index. This index is also an indicator that evaluates the strength of the price of a security that you may be interested in. The figure indicated is relative and provides traders with a picture of how the stock is performing relative to the markets. You will need information regarding volatility and past performance. All traders, regardless of their trading styles, need this useful indicator. Using this relative evaluation tool gives you a figure that lies between 1 and 100.

Tips on RSI use

The relative strength index is ideally used for identifying divergence. Divergence is used by traders to note trend reversals. We can say that a divergence is a difference between two points. There are bearish and bullish divergent signals. Very large and fast movements at the markets sometimes produce false signals. So, it advisable to always use indicators together with other tools.

You can also use the RSI to identify oversold and overbought conditions. It is crucial that you're able to identify these conditions as you trade because you will easily identify corrections and reversals. Sometimes securities are overbought at the markets, when this situation occurs, it means that there is a probable trend reversal and usually

54

the emerging trend is bearish. This is often a market correction. Basically, when a security is oversold, it signals a correction or bullish trend reversal but when it's overbought, it introduces a bearish trend reversal.

The theory aspect of this condition requires a ratio of 70:30. This translates to 70% overvalued or over purchased and 30% undervalued or oversold. Though, in some cases, you might be safer going for the 80/20 ratio just to prevent false breakouts.

Volume

When trading, volume is a crucial indicator and constitutes a major part of any trading strategy. As a trader, you want to always target stocks with high volumes as these are considered liquid. So many traders, especially new ones, disregard volume and look at other indicators instead.

While volume is great for liquidity purposes, it is also desirable for trend. A good trend should be supported by volume. A large part of any stock's volume should constitute part of any trend for it to be a true and reliable trend.

Most of the time traders will observe a trend based on price action. You need to also be on the lookout for new money which means additional players and volume. If you note significant volumes contributing to a trend, then you can be confident about your analysis. Even when it comes to a downtrend, there should be enough volumes visible for it to be considered trustworthy. A lack of volume simply means a stock has either been undervalued or overvalued.

Accumulation and Distribution Line

Another indicator that is widely used by swing traders is the accumulation/distribution line. This indicator is generally used to track the money flow within a security. The money that flows into and out of a stock provides useful information for your analysis.

The accumulation/distribution indicator compares very well with another indicator, the OBV, or the on-balance-volume indicator. The difference in this case is that it considers the trading range as well as the closing price of a stock. The OBV only considers the trading range for a given period.

When a security closes out close to its high, then the accumulation/distribution indicator will add weight to the stock value compared to closing out close to the mid-point. Depending on your needs and sometimes the calculations, you may want to also use the OBV indicator.

You can use this indicator to confirm an upward trend. For instance, when it's trending upwards, you will observe buying interest because the security will close at a point that is higher than the mid-range. However, when it closes at a point that is lower than the mid-range, then volume is indicated as negative and this indicates a declining trend.

While using this indicator, you will also want to be on the lookout for divergence. When the accumulation/distribution begins to decline while the price is going up, then you should be careful because this signals possible reversal. On the other hand, if the trend starts to ascend while the price is falling, then this probably indicates a potential price rise soon. It's advisable to ensure that your internet and other connections are extremely fast especially when using these indicators as time is of essence.

The average directional index, ADX

Another tool or indicator that is widely used by swing traders is the average-directional-index, the ADX. This indicator is basically a trend indicator and its purpose is largely to check the momentum and strength of a trend. A trend is believed to have directional strength if the ADX value is equal to or higher than 40. The directional could be upwards or downward based on the general price direction. But when the ADX value is below 20, then we can say that there is no trend or there is one, but it's weak and unreliable.

You will notice the ADX line on your charts as it is the main line and is often black in color. There are other lines that can be shown additionally. These lines are DI-and DI+

and in most cases are green and red in color, respectively. You can use all the three lines to track both the momentum and the trend direction.

Aroon Technical Indicator

Another useful indicator that you can use is the Aroon indicator. This is a technical indicator designed to check if a financial security is trending. It also checks to find out whether the security's price is achieving new lows or new highs in some time.

You can also use this technical indicator to discover the onset of a new trend. It features two distinct lines which are the Aroon down line and the Aroon up line. A trend is noted when the Aaron up line traverses across the Aaron down line. To confirm the trend, observe the Aroon up line at the 100-point mark and remaining there.

The reverse holds water as well. When the Aroon down line cuts below the Aaron up line, then we can presume a downward trend. To confirm this, we should note the line getting close to 100-point mark and staying there.

This popular trading tool comes with a calculator which you can use to determine several things. If the trend is bullish or bearish, then the calculator will let you know. The formulas used to determine this refer to the most recent highs and lows. When the Aroon values are high then recent values were used and when they are low, the values used were less recent. Typical Aroon values vary between o and 100. Figures that are close to 0 indicate a weak trend while those closer to 100 indicate a strong trend.

The bullish and bearish Aroon indicators can be converted into one oscillator. This is done by making the bearish one range from 0 to -100 while the bullish one ranges from 100 to 0. The combined indicator will then oscillate between 100 and -100. 100 will indicate a strong trend, 0 means there is no trend while -100 implies a negative or downward trend.

Chapter 8: What Are Stock Market Exchanges?

Stock market exchanges are organized, regulated financial markets, where securities (shares, bonds, and notes) are bought and sold at prices dictated by the law of supply and demand. Stock exchanges fundamentally serve as:

1. Primary markets where corporations, municipalities, governments, and other incorporated bodies are permitted to raise capital by offering productive ventures to investors.

2. Secondary markets where investors can meet to buy and sell securities from or to other investors, thus reducing risk and maintaining liquidity.

Stock exchanges compel the participants (all listed and trading parties) to follow their statutory requirements, stringent rules, and listing requirements.

In the older exchanges, trades are conducted on the 'trading floor' of the exchange. The traders use the open outcry system wherein they shout orders and instructions. In the modern exchanges, the trades are done in a more peaceful, well-behaved manner. The business is usually conducted online or over the phone.

All through the trading day, buyers enter competitive bids and sellers enter competitive orders. In some European exchanges, they utilize a method that uses round-robin calls. This method is called 'periodic auction'.

Role of a Stock Exchange

The stock exchange has different roles and each one is highly important in helping the country achieve economic development. Stock exchanges can measure and control a country's growth.

The stock exchange is a place where stock trading transactions are executed. The transactions are usually done by your broker or you can trade directly if you hold a membership with that stock market.

Here are some of the significant roles of stock exchanges:

Raise the capital of a corporation or company.

Exchanges make it easy, simple, and convenient for investing public and companies selling shares to meet and go about their business. Stock sellers and buyers only need to visit a stock exchange to achieve their purpose.

Help mobilize savings for investment.

The stock exchanges can help the public get more from their savings by presenting high yielding investments. The higher yield can be beneficial to both stockholders and the national economy.

Ensure equality in profit sharing.

Stock exchanges make sure both casual and professional stock investors are able to get their fair share of profit.

Facilitate the growth of a company.

The exchanges can help many companies attain the needed expansion and growth through fusion or acquisition.

Create investment prospects for small investors.

Small investors can buy small number of shares so they too can have a chance to participate in the large companies' growth.

Provide good corporate governance.

Companies must follow the stock exchanges' stringent rules if they want to get listed. Due to such rigidness, listed public companies have able to gain better record management as compared with privately held companies.

Aid the government in raising capital for projects related to the development of a region.

The exchanges can help government to raise fund for projects or activities that can help make the region prosper. An investor can take advantage of the bonds that the government issues. Buying a government bond means lending money to the government. The bonds are more secure, and sometimes there are also tax benefits that can be gathered from the said transaction.

Serve as economy's barometer.

The stock exchange has the capability to regulate the fluctuations in stock prices.

How do Companies Get Listed in the Stock Exchange?

To get listed in the stock exchange, a company must first conduct an Initial Public Offering or IPO. When conducting an IPO, a company sells shares to public shareholders or the primary market. The shareholders who would like to sell their shares and buyers who seek good stocks to buy usually go to the stock exchange.

The IPO Process

The entire process of turning a private company into a public one can be time consuming but still worth it. A company may need to hire an investment bank, which will take care of the initial public offering.

While it's true that individual investors from IPO are initially the ones to provide the company with additional capital, the investment bank is the one that usually finances the transaction. The investment bank provides the capital to the issuing company prior to going public with their stocks.

Here is the step by step IPO process:

1. The company that needs to get listed in the stock exchange must hire an underwriter or investment bank. The underwriter will help and guide the company through its IPO process.

2. The company is required to register with Securities and Exchange Commission (SEC) and notify the agency that the company would like to go public. It's best to have an attorney to avoid misinterpretation of statements or information.

3. The company must write a detailed record regarding its history, growth potential, services, products, and market share. A list regarding risk disclosures (must comply with the regulations of SEC) must be included. The company must also maintain factual and accurate information regarding their operations and financial status. The company must work with their attorney to make sure that they comply with SEC regulations.

4. The company must establish good relationship with the brokerage houses as well as investment bank, which can provide a lot of help in the success of the IPO process.

5. There is a need to promote the IPO with prospective shareholders at media outlets and brokerage houses all over the country. Such a move can create noise about the company's offer even before the IPO is approved by SEC.

6. Respond to SEC's queries without delay and obtain the approval of SEC. The company and its attorney must review all the documents before submission.

7. Determine the IPO price.

The company may decide to go public through a stock exchange, such as National Association of Securities Dealers Automated Quotations (NASDAQ), New York Stock Exchange (NYSE), Toronto Stock Exchange, and others. The different stock exchanges may ask for additional requirements that the company must fulfill.

The Different Stock Exchanges

Here are some of the leading stock exchanges in the world:

New York Stock Exchange (NYSE)

NYSE is located in New York City, and was founded on May 17, 1792. The registered owner of NYSE is Intercontinental Exchange. It has listed market capitalization of $19.6 trillion in 2016. It occupies the top spot in the list of world's largest stock exchange.

When trading in NYSE, specialists usually grace the trading floors of the exchange with their presence. Every specialist handles a stock that they can deal with utmost confidence. These specialists won't allow the electronic-only exchanges to threaten their existence. They continuously enhance their skills and try to be more competent.

The NYSE is still the most prestigious and largest exchange in the world. Companies that are listed on the NYSE are expected to possess great credibility, which can attract a lot of investors. Most investors know that these companies must first meet NYSE's initial listing requirements before they can get listed. They must also be able to comply with NYSE's annual maintenance requirements, such as the companies' price per share must be $4 and above and should have more than $40 million market capitalization.

National Association of Securities Dealers Automated Quotations (NASDAQ)

NASDAQ is located in New York City, and was founded on February 4, 1971. The registered owner of NASDAQ is NASDAQ, Inc. It has listed market capitalization of $7.8 trillion in 2016. It occupies the second spot in the list of world's largest stock exchange.

NASDAQ is an electronic exchange, and it also sometimes called "screen-based" because buying and selling can be accomplished using a computer and telecommunications network. Dealers must carry their own stock inventory. They prepare themselves to buy and sell NASDAQ stocks, and they also need to post their bid and ask prices.

The listing requirements of NASDAQ are like that of NYSE. Companies that would like to get listed on NASDAQ should maintain a minimum price of $4 per stock share. If a company fails to maintain the requirements of NASDAQ, it can be delisted.

Toronto Stock Exchange (TSX)

Toronto Stock Exchange (TSX) is located in Toronto, Ontario, Canada, and was officially founded on October 25, 1861. The registered owner of TSX is TMX Group.

It has listed market capitalization of $2 trillion in 2016. It occupies the fourth spot in the 2016 list of growing stock value.

TSX is Canada's largest stock exchange. It was established in 1852, but the TSX's official foundation happened on 1861. The owner of TSX is TMX, which is owned by Maple Group Acquisition Corporation.

The TSX became the second (Montreal Exchange was the first at that time) official stock exchange in Canada in 1878 when the Act of the Ontario Legislature formally incorporated it. Back then, only 18 securities were listed, and daily trading was limited only to half-hour sessions.

TSX was referred to as TSE until 2001, and still maintained the full name Toronto Stock Exchange. TSX is North America's third largest stock exchange in terms of capitalization. In 2009, it merged with Montreal Stock Exchange and the parent company became known as TMX Group. TSX trades are done electronically since they abolished their trading floor in 1997.

London Stock Exchange (LSE)

London Stock Exchange (LSE) is in London, England. In 1571, it was known as the Royal Exchange and London Stock Exchange was officially founded in 1801. The registered owner of LSE is the London Stock Exchange Group. It has listed market capitalization of $3.5 trillion in 2016. It occupies the fifth spot in the 2016 list of world's largest stock exchange.

Although LSE has been around for hundreds of years, the London Stock Exchange Group that officially owned it was only established in 2007. Milan Stock Exchange and LSE merged in 2007. LSE once had a failed merger with TSX.

Shanghai Stock Exchange (SSE)

Shanghai Stock Exchange (SSE) is in Shanghai, China, and was founded on November 26, 1990. It has listed market capitalization of $4.1 trillion in 2016. It occupies the fourth spot in the 2016 list of world's largest stock exchange. It also occupies the second spot in the list of Asia's largest stock exchanges.

SSE is the world's largest stock exchange that is still controlled and owned by a government. It is mainland China's largest stock exchange that operates as a non-profit entity. The China Securities Regulatory Commission is the one responsible for SSE's operation. It's considered one of the most restrictive among the major stock exchanges when it comes to trading and listing standards. You also need to learn some stock market terminologies to make things easier.

Chapter 9: Understanding Diversification

Diversification is a very significant strategy for investing. As a financial term, it means simply distributing your investments in various industries for stocks, combining different financial assets, and creating a mix of these assets that will enable you to meet your investment goals. But in the world of investing, diversification refers to a very specific strategy of investment—the careful selection of assets that would react in different ways to a particular event. So far, we have identified the events that create market volatility and make investing in the stock market a risky endeavor. A portfolio combines shares with ETFs, REITs, trust funds, bonds, and other assets, but if not done properly, it can combine assets that react the same way or in a similar manner to events in the economy.

With diversification, you put together stocks that fit together like a cogwheel so that every drop in the price of a particular asset is counterbalanced by a rise in the value of another. When the price of oil stocks go up, you can almost be assured that airlines, which will now charge more because oil is selling at higher prices, will be doing less business. Their stocks will most probably drop. The inverse is also very true. Having a stock from each sector in your stock portfolio means that your portfolio will always be balanced out whatever happens in either industry. If the oil and airlines industries combination doesn't appeal to you, then you can trade out oil with railway companies. When anything happens to reduce traveler confidence in the airline industry, railroads experience a surge in travelers and vice versa.

Another fantastic combination of assets that can help you keep your portfolio balanced out is that of stocks and bonds in general terms. Stocks normally drop in price when interest rates climb, a time when the price of bonds climbs. Most investment gurus define diversification as simply ensuring that you don't keep all your eggs in a single basket. This hypothetical basket represents the geographical location, economic sector, and investment type.

Pros and Cons

The benefits of diversification have been addressed at length above. The main reason why we diversify, however, is that it allows you to secure your investments against market volatility and keep your investment stable.

Another advantage of diversification is that it allows you to cover your bases. By thinking about the risk quotient of assets before choosing to invest in them, we can identify potential hurdles before they become too problematic. For one thing, diversification forces us to think about our risk tolerance, which is the foundation for a good portfolio.

One of the biggest drawbacks to diversification comes from a very curious aspect of the diversification process—choosing your assets. With so many assets to choose from, you might get stumped, unable to choose between different assets.

Another disadvantage of diversification is that it demands that you select stocks from different, unrelated industries. Choosing between a few good assets in the same market sector leaves the chance that the asset you forfeit is the best one of them all and you can only watch as it rises in price and you cannot take advantage. The opportunity cost of choosing one stock over another could be very demoralizing.

Another con to excessive diversification is that the balancing out of assets in your portfolio whereby a rise in one asset is met by a corresponding drop in other leads to average returns. The cost of trying too hard to ensure that your portfolio will bring you no losses is the fact that you can never make much money. The former hinders the latter.

Another drawback to diversification is that you are more likely to incur massive costs while trying to balance it out by constantly buying and selling.

So, is it worthwhile diversifying?

The answer is *definitely!* A diversified portfolio is a huge confidence booster because it assures you that your investment is secure. The only problems arise when you overly diversify or micromanage the risks associated with each asset on your portfolio. Diversification goes along with portfolio management. The more closely you monitor your portfolio, the better you can diversify. If you think the passive style of portfolio management does not pay enough attention to the assets in your portfolio, a midway point between active and passive portfolio management can allow you to hit the sweet spot for the best results for you.

Chapter 10: Where to Buy and Sell Stocks

The use of shares, whether it is to collect dividends or to speculate on their listing, is an increasingly widespread and interesting practice. The risk of loss is always present but depending on the way you buy and sell your shares; this risk can be reduced. If you're wondering how to buy and sell the shares of large listed companies online, here are some explanations that may interest you.

Transacting with Online Banks

The easiest way to buy and sell shares is to go through one of the placement products offered by banks and, in particular, by online banks. Thanks to the 100% online operation of these banks, you can easily pass your purchase and sale orders directly via the internet without moving.

The advantages of this system are numerous because it's your bank that will be taken care of executing your orders and then buying and selling your shares. To take advantage of stock market shares through these systems, you must underwrite an Investment Plan in Shares, a securities account or life insurance which are the main banking products on the stock market. The only drawback of this method concerns the expenses that may be higher than those that you would have to pay if you bought and sold the shares yourself.

But bank commissions rarely exceed 4%.

One of the main advantages of bank placement products is that your purchases and sales of shares are supervised by market intermediaries and you can benefit from advice.

Transacting with Online Brokers

Another method is to contact an online mediator. Their operation is almost identical to that of online banks with the difference that you do not enjoy assistance and advice, but at the same time, the costs are lower because you decide for yourself what actions to buy or sell.

These online brokers also allow trading through stock market shares without having to buy them. To do this, you need to speculate on the evolution of their value. The tools that allow you to proceed in this way are CFDs.

Ultimately, there are several methods to buy and sell shares on the internet. Before deciding on one or other of these solutions, take care to correctly evaluate the commissions involved as well as your level of knowledge on the stock exchange. Depending on these criteria, each of these two methods has different advantages. It is also good to understand the quotation system of an action to be able to speculate on this type of assets.

The Cost of Purchase or Sales of Shares

To answer this question, it's essential to define the strategy that will be adapted to buy or sell your shares.

If you own a stock portfolio through the intermediation of a stock market product, each investment in the purchase or sale will have a cost corresponding to the expenses called "brokerage expenses" These expenses can take various forms and involve different costs depending on the share traded (national, European, or international market), the amount of the transaction carried out, and, obviously, the intermediary. Things are simpler for online trading and expenses are generally lower. In fact, to be sure, there are no defined brokerage fees for the sale or purchase of shares on the Stock Exchange from a trading platform through CFDs. Obviously, the mediator has a remuneration, however, but in a different and more transparent form: the spread is applied.

The spread corresponds to a small difference between the real quotation of an asset and the quotation of purchase or sale. As a result, when buying shares, the purchase price will be slightly higher than the real price of the asset in question, and in the case of a sale of shares, the selling price will be slightly lower than the real asset price.

Shares that Can Be Bought or Sold Online

For some years now, the offer of mediators in terms of CFDs on shares has been considerably enriched, and it is now possible to access many stocks from the trading platforms made available to the general public.

Chapter 11: The FOREX Market vs. the Stock Market

Trading FOREX can be a very interesting hobby for people in the current world. This form of a thrilling kind of hobby can be a great source of generating revenue. To lighten up people's lives, over five trillion US dollars are traded in a day. To formally understand the trade, the process is divided into three namely learning basics terminologies in FOREX, opening of an online FOREX brokerage account and starting the trade.

Understanding basic FOREX terminology

The first two terminologies an individual is supposed to understand are the base currency and quote currency. During the FOREX trade, two currencies are always traded. The currency that is being sold is the base currency. The currency being bought is the quote currency. For a person to buy the quote currency, they will be guided by the foreign exchange rates. The foreign exchange rates help a person to know how much they will have to spend.

There are two positions in the process of trading currencies. A person can choose to take a long term or short-term position. A long-term position involves a person buying the base currency and in turn selling the quote currency. On the other hand, buying the base currency and selling the base currency is referred to a trader taking a short-term position. The trader always has a price which they can willingly buy the base currency in exchange to get quote currency. This price is always known as a bid fee.

Bid prices can change during the process of broking currencies. This leads to the rise of an asking price. It is the price an individual can sell the base currency in return to gain the quote currency. Bid price mostly is the best price available in the market a person can buy the other currency. The difference between the asked price and the bid price is known as a spread.

Reading the FOREX quote

There are two numbers an individual will observe in the FOREX quote. The numbers present include the bid price and the asking price. The bid price is always situated on the left side while the asking price is always situated on the right side.

Descending on what currency a person wants to buy and sell

This process starts with a person predicting an economy. An individual can take a common economy like the United States of America economy. If the the US economy is declining, the situation is bad for the American dollar since it will depreciate in terms of value. Consequently, the situation will lead to people offloading the dollar in exchange for the other forms of currency with strong economies.

The individual can look at a country trading position to know which currency to buy and sell. The better country to look at is that with a high amount of goods that are inconsistent demand. There are high possibilities for such a country to have high numbers of exports and thus make more money from international and local trade. The phenomenon will be a strong boost to a country and in turn, boosting the currency. The information favoring such a country gives a trader the best currency to invest in.

The decision over which currency to buy and sell can be determined by the political temperatures of a country. The most crucial times are during the elections in a country. The currency is approximated to rise if a person winning the election has an agenda aligning to favorable fiscal policies. The currency can be favorable to buy if the regulations on economic growth are loosened. The action usually leads to an increase in the value of a country's currency.

Economic reports of a country can also help a person in making the decision on which currency to buy and sell. An individual can choose to focus on a country's Gross Domestic Income or a country's Per Capita Income. Other information that can be critical includes the employment rate and inflation rate. This critical information will provide a trader with accurate information about the value of the currency to buy and sell.

Learning how to calculate profits

The process involves a person's ability to be able to measure the value change in two currencies. Pip measures the difference between the two traded currencies. One pip is usually equated to 0.0001change in value. A good example can be drawn from an exchange of the Euro to the American dollar. If the trade of EUR/USD shifts from 2.646 to 2.647, the value of the currency is said to have increased by ten pips. The next step involves an individual multiply the pips numbers their account with the current exchange rates. The value got will help an individual know if he has made a gain or a decrease in his account.

Opening of Online FOREX Brokerage Account

Researching of different brokerages

There are several factors an individual is supposed to consider while choosing his brokerage. These factors to consider include:

Going out for the experience. This should be the main consideration when choosing a brokerage individual or a company. The person or company is decided on is supposed to have a minimum experience of ten years in the market. The experience will be able to help a person to know the company is on track. Experience also indicates the company, or an individual is good at taking care of their clients.

One is supposed to ensure that the brokerage is regulated. The regulation of brokerages is mostly done by the chief oversight body. It's very pleasing if a broker chose on has a total submission to the government. The situation gives an individual reassurance on broker transparency and honesty. There are several oversight bodies across the globe, and they include.

United Kingdom; Financial Conduct Authority

Switzerland; Swiss Federal Banking Institution.

Australia; Australian Securities and Investment Commission.

The types of available products by the broker are also another factor for an individual to consider. There are some factors that help an individual to know if the brokerage has a wide business reach and a large client base. One of the determining factors these occurrences is also trading securities and commodities.

Someone interested in the FOREX market is supposed to be a careful reader of reviews. It is because some dishonest brokers can write reviews that are false to build a good brand for themselves. These reviews written help an individual to get the flavor of the broker. That being said, one is supposed to take these brokers with a granule of the brackish.

Visiting the website of a broker is not supposed to be left out. This website is supposed to have a good professional look. The links provided on the website are supposed to be functional also. If there are any doubts on the website, one is supposed to steer clear from the broker.

Checking on the transactional cost of each trade is also advantageous to a person interested to be successful in FOREX trade. They are supposed to check how much the bank will charge them for wiring funds into their FOREX account.

You should be able to focus on the essentials. These include focusing on good clientele support and transactions that are easy and transparent. You should be attracted to a broker with a good reputation.

Requesting information about opening an account

There are two forms of account an individual can open to be able to trade in the FOREX market. You can choose to open a personal account or a managed account. Having a personal account will let you manage your account yourself. On the other hand, having a managed account tasks the broker with the execution of trade on behalf of the individual.

Filling out the correct paperwork

There are several ways the appropriate paperwork can be filled. You can choose to order the paperwork by mail services. The other method will entail downloading the papers from the internet in the form of a PDF file. The next step will involve you checking the transaction charges by the bank for transferring funds to your brokerage account. This fee is essential because it affects the profit calculation in the FOREX trade.

Activation of the account

The most common occurrence entails the broker sending the activation link to your email. The link sent always contains guidelines that help you start.

Starting Trading

Analysis of the market

Market analysis is always the first step while starting to trade in the FOREX market. There are several ways you can use to analyze the market. They include:

Technical analysis: This entails the use of chats or historical data. These forms will help a FOREX trader to be able to predict the movement of currency basing his thought on the previous events. These data can be obtained from several sources. The main form sources include from the brokerage or the MetaTrader which is a common platform for those in the FOREX trade.

Fundamental analysis: This form of analysis involves taking a keen look at the key areas in a country's economy. The information from these fundamental areas form a key to a person's trading choice.

Sentimental analysis: This form of market analysis is highly subjective. Using this form of market analysis, you will get a good analysis of the market mood. This will enable you to know if the market is bullish. It's very difficult to put a finger on the sentiment of the market. Although, you are capable of making very good guesses that influence their trade.

Determining your margin

This is highly dependable on the broker's strategy in place. You can make investments of small amounts of money and still be able to make huge trades in the FOREX market. An example can be used of someone with a desire to trade one hundred units at one percent margin. This will make the broker put one thousand American dollars in their account to act as security. If they make the gains, it will add in their account. On the other hand, losses will deduct from the your account from its value. Such occurrences have made individuals invest 2% of the funds in a specific pair currency.

Placing your order

You at this point can place orders of various kinds. These orders include:

- Market order: This order includes you using the market order to instruct your broker to buy or sell at the present market rates.

- Limit orders: This point entails you instructing your broker to trade at a precise price. You can sell the currency when it lowers to a certain price or you can buy when it gains up to a certain price.

Stop orders; this order involves two of the options. You can decide to buy currency above the present value in the market. On the other hand, you can choose to sell currency below the present market value.

Watching your profit and loss

At this point, you are warned from becoming emotional. It is because the market is very volatile in most cases. You will observe lots of ups and downs. Hence, you are supposed to be firm with their strategy in the market. This will enable you to see profits coming overtime if you are confident in your strategy.

Chapter 12: Risk Management in Stock Market

Stock market risk usually refers to the risk that investors won't be able to make profits or even recover their costs after entering the stock market. It's mainly reflected in the fact that after investors buy a stock at a certain price and when the stock price drops sharply as a result, they cannot sell the stock at a lower price than when they bought resulting in a hold-up phenomenon.

Risk refers to the possibility of loss or damage. Judging from the definition of risk, there are mainly two kinds of stock investment risks: one is the loss of investors' income and principal; The other is the loss of investors' income and purchasing power of principal.

Stock investment risk has obvious duality, that is, its existence is objective, absolute, subjective and relative. It is both inevitable and controllable. Investors' control of stock risks is to minimize the risk-bearing cost by using a series of investment strategies and technical means according to the duality of risks.

Types of Stock Market Risks

People often say that in the stock market, ordinary people's intuition sometimes surpasses the theories of experts. The founder of Adam's theory which is still valid, after years of enthusiastic research on technical analysis, finally rejected all his research results because he believed that the trend in the stock market could not be predicted. All analysis tools had inevitable defects. Any analysis tool could not predict the trend of the stock market absolutely and accurately.

All the data and charts in the technical analysis only represent the past and reflect the information of the past. You can only predict probability of something happening. Compared with the unpredictable stock market, nothing is impossible. For technical analysis, shareholders should look at it dialectically, combine the results of technical analysis with actual trends, and follow the trend to avoid maximum risks.

Emotional and Person Risk

First and foremost, you can control the risks to your investments that come from personal factors. These include fear, impatience, and greed. Emotions like these can be hard to control but learning to take charge of them is essential if you're going to be a successful investor. When real money is on the line, these emotions can become strong and overpowering. You must not let that happen.

Risk of Loss of Capital

Obviously, financial risk is something you face when investing. Theoretically, there is a chance that you'll lose all the money you invest in the stock market. This can happen if you tie your fate to a small number of companies. Several well-known companies like Lumber Liquidators, Bear-Stearns, and GM have either had major problems or gone completely under. Investors may have lost large sums in the process. The way to deal with this is to avoid investing in a small number of companies. Later in the chapter, we will investigate diversification as an investment strategy.

Market and Economic Risk

Some factors are beyond your control, and the economy inevitably cycles through slowdowns and downturns. The market will cycle along with the economy, and experience crashes when the economy may be doing fine overall. This happened in 1987, for example.

While these factors aren't under your control, how you react to them is. As we discussed in the section on emotional risk, you should not panic when there is a downturn. Remain levelheaded, and use this as a buying opportunity. They are always followed by a brighter day; your job is to have the patience to wait for it to arrive.

Interest Rate Risk

Changing interest rates can impact the markets. Although this is a book about stock market investing, you should have some awareness of how bond markets work. You should also be aware that investor money can flow back and forth between bond and stock markets depending on conditions.

Political Risk and Government

Government and politics can create big risks in the stock market. International events can cause market crashes, and these days even a tweet from the President can cause markets to rise and fall. Lately, some politicians have been discussing breaking up the big tech companies. Others are talking about investigating them. Such talk and actions can have a negative impact on the markets. Part of your job as an investor is to keep a close eye on the news. You're going to want to know what's happening so that you can adjust if necessary.

Inflation Risk

Inflation hasn't been high in decades. Although, in the late 1970s inflation rates were routinely in the double digits. Hopefully, that isn't going to be something that happens anytime soon, because high inflation rates can eat your returns alive. If the stock market is appreciating at 7% per year, but inflation is 14%, you can see that it's like having debt but investing in stocks – it's a losing proposition. Right now, inflation risk is very low, but you'll want to have some awareness of it and always keep tabs on it. High inflation rates tend to go hand-in-hand with high-interest rates, since the Federal Reserve will raise rates to try and slow down inflation. That means that bonds might become more attractive when inflation gets out of control.

Taxes and Commissions

Finally, we have the risk imposed by taxes. Of course, we are all going to be hit with taxes no matter where our money comes from. However, you need to consider the taxes that you're going to pay when it comes to any gains you realize on the stock market. Part of being a successful investor is understanding how much your taxes are cutting into your profits. If you're investing for the long-term, it will be less of an issue. But keep in mind that taxes can really eat into short-term trades. Frequent, short-term traders also face risk from commissions and fees. If you execute a lot of trades, the commissions can add up. This isn't an issue for long term investors.

Risk vs. Return

One of the fundamental trade-offs that an investor will make is a risk vs. return. Generally, the higher the risk, the greater the *possibility* of good returns. In 1998, Amazon was a high-risk investment. While it had potential, major bookstores like Borders and Barnes & Noble dominated the space. Amazon was on shaky ground at the time, and another company could have come in and competed successfully for online book sales. That never happened, and Amazon ended up dominating book sales and expanding widely across retail and into cloud computing. That risk has translated into massive returns. A $10,000 investment in 1998 would be worth more than $1 million today.

But hindsight is 20/20. Today, there are similar opportunities all around us, but it's hard to know which ones are going to end up being successful over the long term. If you're an aggressive investor, part of your job is going to be estimating which companies are the best bets for the future.

Risk vs. Return also plays a role in emerging markets. These countries may experience massive GDP growth year after year since they have lots of room to grow. Domestic companies that are growing with their economies can offer remarkable returns. But there are many risks. Rapid growth can often evaporate with major downturns. Stability is lower in emerging markets; you could face complete loss of capital.

Managing Risk

There are a few time-tested strategies that have been developed that help manage risk. They even minimize the kinds of risk you'll face that are completely out of control. That could include anything from a terrorist attack to interest rate changes.

These strategies are simple and easy to understand. The problem is that in practice, many investors fail to follow them, and instead let their decision making be guided by emotions. You might end up following that path as well. However, we are going to give you the tools you need to avoid it. It's up to you whether you utilize them or not.

<u>Dollar Cost Averaging</u>

The first strategy seeks to avoid being impacted by the ups and downs of the market. You don't know when you are buying at the top of a market or the bottom. None of us has a crystal ball, but what we can do is average out our investments over the long-term. You can do this using a technique called dollar cost averaging, which is simply buying shares at regular intervals – completely ignoring price fluctuations. Most ups and downs in the stock market are just noise. So, you should avoid worrying about them as much as possible. And we've already noted that stock goes up and down with bull and bear markets. Using dollar cost averaging, you remove the stress (and hence the emotion) that is associated with these fluctuations. The costs are averaged out because sometimes you'll be buying when prices are low, even though at other times you'll be buying when prices are relatively high.

Those short-term ups and downs don't matter over the long-term. Whether Amazon

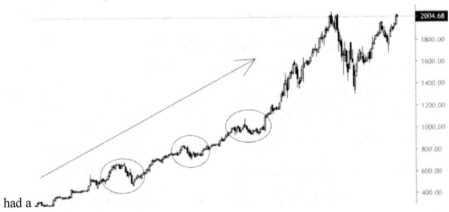

had a

long gain 4 years ago or not won't matter to the investor using dollar cost averaging. All that matters is the long-term trend – and regularly purchasing shares along the way. Looking at the chart below, we've used an arrow to show Amazon's long-term trend and circled a few of the short-term fluctuations that at the time, caused a great deal of

85

angst and anxiety. Traders probably tried to profit from them. But look how small they are, compared to the overall picture.

Diversification

A lot of people don't like to hear about this one since financial advisors are constantly shoving it down people's throats. But diversification remains one of the most basic strategies in stock market investing. The problem is most investors don't diversify enough.

Volatility

Prices are moving up and down, dramatically swinging between highs and lows. That's what volatility is. It can be measured in terms of the frequency of price changes and the magnitude. The higher the differences between the highs and lows, and the more frequently stock prices fluctuate, the higher the volatility.

Traders like high volatility. That means there are more opportunities for stock prices to trend in their favor. An options trader, for example, likes a high volatility stock because, over the lifetime of the option, the probability is increased that the share price will move to a favorable position, even if it's just for a short time.

To quantify the volatility of a stock, you'll want to look at a quantity investors call *Beta*. This compares the volatility of any given stock to the entire market.

Master the professional knowledge of securities

In order to avoid risks and gain profits from investments, new investors must do the following two things before trading stocks.

(1) To understand the risks and traps of the stock market, one must understand the corresponding stock knowledge in detail.

(2) According to certain professional knowledge, analyze and avoid these risks and traps.

Avoid mistakes in stock market operation

Although many ordinary investors are cautious and cautious after entering the market, there are still a lot of assets that are lost as the index rises and falls. This is mainly because many investors have big or small mistakes in actual operations. Let's look at what common mistakes investors have in the stock market.

(1) There is no stop loss concept.

The setting of stop-loss and stop-gain is quite necessary. Many investors always fantasize about buying at the lowest point and selling at the highest point. They don't know the stock market clearly. They must stop-loss when breaking the position.

(2) Buy only cheap stocks.

It's necessary to know that the low price of the stock price is only compared with the previous period. If the upside is too heavy, the momentum of the stock rise isn't enough to cross the resistance zone, and the stock price is also difficult to rise. Buying such stocks blindly only based on the low price will bring great losses to investors.

Predict the market.

Many investors like to "predict" stock prices through technical analysis. In fact, for technical analysis, investors should look at it dialectically, combine the results of technical analysis with actual trends, and follow the trend to avoid risks as much as possible.

When the quilt cover is worn, it will be sold after it is removed.

Technically, it isn't advisable to wait for the deep-seated stocks to be unwound. Investors cannot passively wait for the results. Active measures are the right path.

Tracking the purchase of active stock.

Usually you need to buy in a short time of 15 minutes before and after the rise in active stock. When ordinary investors find active stock, they often miss the best buying opportunity.

Analyze the environment and seize the opportunity.

As the saying goes, "when choosing stocks is not as good as when choosing them", choosing a good investment timing can reduce the possibility of the selected stocks falling and effectively avoid systemic risks. To grasp the general investment opportunity, investors can pay attention to the following two details.

Political changes.

Political factors can easily affect social stability. If regime change brings social unrest, the stock market will fall.

Price rise.

Under normal circumstances, after the price rises, the stock price of the corresponding type generally rises, and prices fell, and the corresponding share price fell.

Investors should pay due attention to such large environments as political events, inflation and price changes, cultivate enthusiasm for state affairs and international current affairs, understand the current situation and trend of national policy implementation and economic development. They should also have a keen judgment on the impact of macroeconomic changes on the economic situation.

Choose the right investment method

After all, the stock market is a high-risk place. Even if you adopt more skills and learn more theories, you'll inevitably encounter risks. Choosing the right investment method can effectively avoid various risks in the stock market.

Adopt diversified investment methods.

Using different investment methods for different stocks according to their characteristics can achieve the purpose of dispersing risks through diversified investment methods. Investors should not only adopt a single investment mode, but also combine long-term, medium-term and short-term investment modes.

Diversify investment and reserve enough spare funds.

The purpose of diversification is to diversify risks, reduce risks and avoid risks. Its method is to combine different securities into investment portfolios. Of course, the risk is not the more dispersed the better, but should be enough. Retail investors with small principal should be relatively concentrated, which is relatively low in cost and easy to form economies of scale.

Formulate a reasonable investment plan

In fact, when many investors buy stocks, they usually buy randomly to get a variety of different stocks in their own accounts, but the result is often to buy many loss-making stocks. In view of the different age, occupation, income and economic conditions of each investor, each investor should have his own unique investment plan.

- According to their own investment ability they should choose a strategy.

- Determine the investment scale according to their financial resources.

- Determine the investment cycle according to the available time and funds.

- Decide the investment direction and choose the investment object according to their tolerance to risks.

- Make investment plans according to the energy of investors.

- Be vigilant against unhealthy advisory bodies.

Most stock investors across the country are losing money, while consulting firms are pocketing large amounts of money easily. The mystery is difficult for outsiders to see.

Most of the stock consulting agencies are following the operation mode of "not speculating in stocks but speculating in stocks". They believe that if everyone believes that there is gold on the mountain across the river, you should not go for gold, but run boats on the river. Consequently, this once again reminds investors that stocks should still believe in themselves and cannot easily believe any gossip!

Pay Attention to Safety in Online Stock Trading

With the development of the Internet and the popularization of computers, more and more people are surfing the Internet, and online stock trading has gradually become a trend. Online trading has many advantages and is easy to operate and isn't subject to geographical restrictions. But when conducting online trading, it is also necessary to pay attention to its safety.

(1) Protect the transaction password. Change the password frequently to ensure that it isn't accessed by others. In addition, when using the Internet to conduct transactions, do not easily download unknown software, so as not to provide opportunities for hackers.

(2) The operation process should be cautious. When online trading fails, you can inquire about the market price or issue trading instructions by phone to avoid unnecessary losses caused by untimely operation.

(3) Withdraw from the trading system. After the transaction is completed, the account must be withdrawn correctly and the transaction system must be shut down, so you don't give anyone a chance to do something.

Conclusion

In the course of your trading experience, you must endeavor to learn from your adventures which is the most effective way to master a skill. Although a mentor or a teacher can help you, you will soon find out that the most influential opinion when trading is your own opinion so you must pay good attention to it and make it better. How can you make your opinion better? You can do this by possessing the right mentality when starting a trade. Whether the trade worked out or not, you must be ready to pick up yourself after losing a trade and focus again on the fact that you can make it again when trading next time. Having said that, you should also consider hiring a coach or get a mentor, someone who can always guide you in times when you experience difficulties in your trades. I hope you have been able to learn some simple yet effective strategies that will help you achieve success in your swing trading journey. Remember, always adhere to your strategy and be disciplined when trading.

I wish the best of luck in your trading.

SCAN ME

CPSIA information can be obtained
at www.ICGtesting.com
Printed in the USA
LVHW022352270521
688666LV00034B/1230

9 781802 936551